43 Team-building Activities

for Key Stage 2

Gavin Middlewood and
Andrew Debenham

 Brilliant Publications

We hope you and your pupils enjoy doing the activities in this book. Brilliant Publications publishes many other books for use in primary schools. To find out more details on any of the titles listed below, please log on to our website: www.brilliantpublications.co.uk.

Title	ISBN
Thinking Strategies for the Successful Classroom 5–7 Year Olds	978-1-905780-03-7
Thinking Strategies for the Successful Classroom 7–9 Year Olds	978-1-905780-04-4
Thinking Strategies for the Successful Classroom 9–11 Year Olds	978-1-905780-05-1
Timely Tasks for Fast Finishers 5–7 Year Olds	978-1-905780-00-6
Timely Tasks for Fast Finishers 7–9 Year Olds	978-1-905780-01-3
Timely Tasks for Fast Finishers 9–11 Year Olds	978-1-905780-02-0
Positively Me – A Self-esteem Programme for Teachers and Pupils	978-1-903853-13-9
Into the Garden of Dreams	978-1-897675-76-2
Smiling Inside, Smiling Outside – Learning to Care for Myself, My Family, My World	978-1-903853-73-3
Brilliant Activities for Gifted and Talented Children	978-1-903853-47-4

Published by Brilliant Publications
Unit 10
Sparrow Hall Farm
Edlesborough
Dunstable
Bedfordshire
LU6 2ES, UK

Sales and stock enquiries:
Tel: 01202 712910
Fax: 0845 1309300
E-mail: brilliant@bebc.co.uk
Website: www.brilliantpublications.co.uk

General information enquiries:
Tel: 01525 222292

The name Brilliant Publications and the logo are registered trademarks.

Written by Gavin Middlewood and Andrew Debenham
Illustrated by Pat Murray
Front cover designed by Z2 Ltd

© Text Gavin Middlewood and Andrew Debenham 2007
© Design Brilliant Publications 2007
ISBN 978-1-903853-57-3

First printed and published in the UK in 2007

Contents

Introduction

What are the aims of this book?

This book aims to provide children with the much-needed opportunity to improve in a range of social and physical skills, in particular interpersonal skills. The development of these skills is targeted within a set of clearly written lesson plans. These have been carefully designed with the busy primary teacher in mind, requiring minimal preparation and equipment. The activities have also been designed to stimulate pupils' imaginations through a series of exciting problems and scenarios.

Each plan begins with a story, which appears on the lesson plans in italic type. From the mountains of the Himalayas to the stormy seas of the Pacific, the children are placed in problematic situations in which they need to work together to find a solution.

Each challenge addresses different social and physical skills at various levels of ability in Key Stage 2.

Where does this fit into the school curriculum?

PE

Outdoor and Adventurous Activities (OAA) is one of the six areas of physical activity that Key Stage 2 children need to engage in within the PE curriculum, along with games, gymnastics, dance, athletics and swimming. The lesson plans in this book enable teachers to access elements of OAA throughout Key Stage 2 within their own school, rather than rely solely on a residential trip.

PSHE

Each activity acknowledges the importance of every individual as a valued part of a team. Successful completion of these tasks requires even the more reticent children to become involved. Some activities necessitate a leader or spokesperson to come to the fore, which can result in dramatic improvements to some pupils' self-esteem.

How can this book be used?

The activities can be planned into the PE and PSHE programmes or can be used by the teacher as stand-alone lessons. The activities have been divided into two main sections: Years 3-4 and Years 5-6. These are purely a guide and activities can be used as the teacher sees appropriate, depending on the class ability.

We have not specified a length of time for the activities as the time needed varies according to the children and teacher involved. The extensions allow the activities to be varied and played again. We have found it worth repeating favourites with variations. As a general guide, the longer activities (as identified on the Contents page) will take one lesson, while you may need to use two of the shorter activities to fill a lesson.

Whilst the individual lessons have valuable outcomes on their own or as part of progressive planning, they have been used to great effect when organized into a competitive format. We have called this 'Team challenge'. Within this framework, teams can compete against each other, either side by side or against the clock. Teams can be awarded tokens according to their finishing position after a particular challenge. They can then accumulate further tokens in subsequent problems (as well as bonus tokens for efficient teamwork, good behaviour etc). When awarding tokens, those made of 'gold' seem to be particularly desirable!

All the activities in this book have been tried and tested many times in schools. However, as with any physical activity, you should do a safety risk assessment prior to carrying out an activity.

Bank-robber balance

Your crack team of burglars is on a secret mission to rob the Bank of England. You've thwarted the guards with your cunning disguises and turned off the security cameras (thanks to the skills picked up in your IT lessons). 'Fingers' Maguire is ready to pick up the cash, but first you and your partner need to deactivate the pressure pad to the vault. This will require the combined balanced weight of two people. Be careful not to let your team 'down'!

Focus
Balance, cooperation
Number of players
2-3
Equipment
Large PE ball
Aim
For the children to work together to maintain a perfect balancing position on the ball.

Instructions

1. The children should begin by experimenting with their cooperative balance on the ball (pressure pad).

2. When they are satisfied that they are ready, they can be timed.

3. For each second that the vault door remains open (the ball is balanced upon), 'Fingers' Maguire can acquire a fictional £1,000 in cash for your squad.

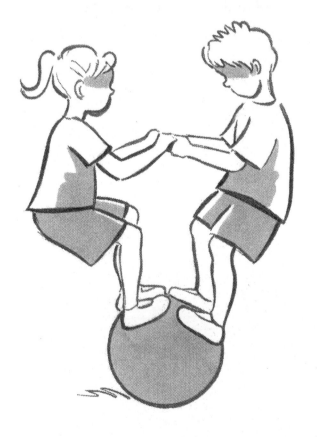

43 Team-building Activities for Key Stage 2
© Gavin Middlewood and Andrew Debenham

The electrical cable

There has been a thunderstorm! Lightning has caused a power cut in your town. You are the broken parts of the electrical cable that normally provides all of the electricity (including the power to your games console!). You must join together to send power to the thousands of people who sit twiddling their thumbs in the dark.

Instructions

1. Each group member holds hands with each other to form a human chain.

2. The first person in the chain holds the hoop in their 'spare' hand.

3. On the teacher's signal, the first child drops the hoop onto their arm, and it is passed along the line through cooperative body movements.

4. The chain must not be broken or the power charge disappears. If the chain breaks, the hoop must be returned to the starting child.

Focus
Cooperation, communication, control of movement
Number of players
3 or more
Equipment
One hoop large enough for a child to squeeze through
Aim
To pass the hoop from one end of the line to the other without breaking the chain.

Extension: This activity can be repeated with a smaller hoop or a larger number of children.

Island SOS

You and your classmates are on a school residential holiday on the remote Scottish island of Jura. Unfortunately, there's been an abseiling accident, with your poor teacher suffering a suspected broken leg. You hear the chug of the coastguard's boat nearby. With slate and chalk in hand, you rush to the cliff's edge to spell out an important message.

Instructions

1. All of the children in the group need to stand on the bench.

2. The teacher provides each child with a letter card.

3. The children must work out what the word is.

4. To complete the task they should help each other move into the correct place on the bench without touching the floor. Children are not allowed to simply exchange letter cards.

Focus
Cooperation, balance, problem-solving
Number of players
4-7
Equipment
Bench
Letter cards (using words from resource sheet on page 57)
Aim
For the group to put themselves in order without falling off the *cliff*.

Extension: This activity can be timed, with specified penalties being incurred each time a child touches the floor.

43 Team-building Activities for Key Stage 2
© Gavin Middlewood and Andrew Debenham

The magnetic spheres

It is the 22nd century AD, and fossil fuels are a thing of the past. As well as using wind, wave and solar power, people of the Earth are travelling using magnetism. Giant magnets at the tops of huge tower blocks are switched on and off in order to draw transportation pods through the sky and carry people to work. Up until now there have been only single pods, but your engineering company, 'McClay Construction', have devised a '2-Pod system'. If you can demonstrate its efficiency to an interested audience of investors then the contract is yours.

Focus
Problem-solving, cooperation
Number of players
4-8
Equipment
2 skipping ropes
2 hoops
Aim
To transport all members of the team across the playing area in the quickest time possible.

Instructions

1. The skipping ropes should be arranged to define the start and finish lines.

2. The children need to stand behind the start line with the two hoops.

3. The teacher needs to explain that they must transport all of their classmates through the air in the two spheres. However, the spheres are magnetized. This means that a part of one hoop must remain in contact with a part of the other hoop at all times. If this contact is lost, then the spheres will fall from the sky!

4. In this demonstration of the '2-pod system', each pod can carry only one person at a time.

Hint: Two children need to travel across together, with one returning with both hoops to collect another passenger.

Raft of robots

It is the year 2045 and robots are in mass production in Britain. You and Dr McClay are transporting two of these robots to multi-millionnaire Lottie Cash, who lives in a huge mansion. This mansion is on an island in the middle of a river for security reasons. Miss Cash has ordered the robots as she is sick of doing the housework. Her state-of-the-art speedboat is currently in repair, so she has left you a small raft to cross the river with. However, the raft is tiny ...

Instructions

1. Cones must be laid out to represent the banks of the river.

2. Each group of four must divide themselves into two scientists and two robots. Players can then distinguish themselves using the coloured bibs.

3. Each group is next given a raft (hoop). Children may travel across the river walking inside of the hoop. However, the raft has limitations. The raft is able to take only the weight of one robot or two scientists at a time, otherwise it will sink.

Focus
Problem-solving
Number of players
4-32 players divided into teams of 4
Equipment
Hoops
Cones
Two different-coloured sets of bibs or bands
Aim
To transport as quickly as possible all 4 members of the group across the *river* within the limitations of the raft.

Hint: First, the raft will need to be taken by the scientists. One will need to stay on the other side, whilst the other will need to bring the raft back. The robots are very clever, by the way, and are able to pilot themselves across the river.

43 Team-building Activities for Key Stage 2
© Gavin Middlewood and Andrew Debenham

Wipeout!

The surf's up and it's time to wax those boards and head for the beach. Competition is likely to be stiff, but there are some awesome prizes on offer! First prize is a week's holiday in Hawaii, so it's the job of your team to make sure that your surfer puts in a smooth performance. Ride the tube, dude!

Instructions

1. Teams must decide which of their members will watch that their surfer doesn't 'wipe out'. The remaining team members must lie on the floor shoulder to shoulder, with arms either by their sides or above their heads.

2. They should then have a PE mat placed on top of them.

3. Upon the teacher's instruction, team members lying on the floor will all execute one full sideways roll in the same direction. This should move the mat without the use of hands.

4. Players can now be informed that in tandem with the PE mat they represent the water. Their *surfer* (toy) will be placed upon its *surfboard* (card) and then upon the mat. It is the players' challenge to move the surfer to the end of the course as smoothly and as quickly as possible.

5. If the surfer falls off his board, he will need to start again in order to impress the judges.

Focus
Cooperation, co-ordination, communication

Number of players
4-32, divided into teams of 4-8 members

Equipment
One PE mat per team
One cuddly toy or action figure per team
One small paper or card surfboard per team

Aim
To organize synchronized rolling in order to efficiently move a PE mat.

Hint: Children should consider how they should order their bodies to avoid undulation.

Alligator swamp

Your band of wildlife experts delves deep into the Everglades searching for evidence of a new species of butterfly. This could be the greatest discovery of modern times! You spot what you are looking for across the swamp. One problem — the swamp is crawling with alligators! Maybe the rope in your backpack and nearby logs can get you there ...

Instructions

1. Players are given the equipment and informed of the task.

2. They must decide as a group how to best use the equipment so that no one is fed to the alligators.

3. When the children have formed their plan, they should attempt to cross the swamp.

Focus
Cooperation, balance
Number of players
3 or more
Equipment
Quoits (one more than the total of children)
2 skipping ropes
Aim
For the group to cross the swamp safely.

Hint: One way that the children can achieve this is by sending a lead member ahead to build a path of logs. The children can then each step upon these, with the last child sending the remaining log to the leader. The positioning of the logs could be controlled by tying them onto the rope.

Extension: The swamp is sinking fast! The task could be completed within a specified time frame.

Dinosaur park

You and your friends have travelled back through time to collect species of dinosaur for your new theme park, 'Dinosaur World'. You are lucky enough to have cornered an exceptionally rare Gatiosaurus! This creature is known for its rattling tail and blinding acid-spray attack. It's in your sights … until it attacks …. Aggghhh! Can you still catch the beast by listening for its rattle?

Focus
Problem-solving
Number of players
15-30
Equipment
Rattle (eg, a plastic cup with beads in it)
Beanbag
Aim
For the *hunters* to capture the *Gatiosaurus* by listening for its *rattle*.

Instructions

1. The class must hold hands to make a circle and create the *park*.

2. The teacher must then choose someone to become the *Gatiosaurus*. This creature can move in any direction that it likes within the park (playing area). However, a beanbag must be held between the knees of the dinosaur at all times. It should also hold the rattle in its hands throughout the activity.

3. Next, a *hunter* should be chosen. The hunter is blindfolded and must attempt to *capture* the Gatiosaurus by tagging it.

4. To help the hunter, every 20-30 seconds the Gatiosaurus must *shake its tail* (rattle).

5. On every third shake of the tail the teacher can choose an additional hunter to join the game and help to catch the Gatiosaurus. This continues until the dinosaur is caught.

Extension: The hunters' task can be made trickier by using a larger playing area.

The curse of Medusa

It is the time of the ancient Greeks and you are the great warrior Perseus. However, your kingdom has been taken away from you and the only way you can win it back is through the magic of Medusa's head! Green and ugly, with hair made from poisonous snakes, Medusa lives on a faraway island. You would normally solve an issue like this with one slash of your sword, but there is one problem – a single look from her eyes will turn you to stone … forever! Somehow you must position a mirror to perfectly reflect her own image back at her so that you will be the victor!

Focus
Non-verbal communication
Number of players
3 or more
Equipment
Blindfolds
Aim
To create a line of identical body shapes whilst blindfolded.

Instructions

1. Groups need to select a Medusa to strike the initial pose at the start of the line. The last person will represent the *mirror*.

2. The remaining children must space out in a straight line.

3. All of the children, except Medusa, must blindfold themselves.

4. Medusa should now strike a pose and hold it for the duration of the challenge.

5. The next child in line (child 2) must feel Medusa's shape and attempt to form that exact same position.

6. The next child in line should feel the position of child 2 and attempt to form that exact same position. This continues down the line.

43 Team-building Activities for Key Stage 2
© Gavin Middlewood and Andrew Debenham

7. Once the mirror has been reached, the children must hold their position, have their blindfolds removed and, finally, judge if the reflection has been a success and whether *Perseus has succeeded*.

Extension: This can be made harder by increasing the group size.

Detective squad

There has been a very serious crime in your local neighbourhood. No one knows who or what was involved. Stranger still, they don't even know where it was exactly. It's all one huge mystery! You are expected to search the place for clues. Can your team of detectives come up with the answers before your neighbouring station?

Instructions

1. The six crime details need to be written on separate pieces of card by the teacher. These should include: criminal's name, age and occupation, crime location, type of crime and weapon used.

2. The pieces of card should be stuck under six separate cones. These must be mixed up with the other cones.

3. The cones are then scattered in a large area.

4. *Squads* should next decide on an order of runners as only one team's detective may leave their *station* at a time.

5. When the teacher instructs that the search can begin, the first detective can leave their station. As soon as they have looked under one cone, they must return to their station, successful or not, ready to tag the next detective.

6. If a detective finds a clue to the crime, they should write the detail down on the squad's report at their station.

7. When the report is complete the squad should together shout 'You're nicked!', and their report can be checked by the teacher.

Focus
Problem-solving, agility, communication
Number of players
4-30 players divided into teams of 2-5
Equipment
20-30 cones or markers
Crime details (on separate pieces of card)
Detective report (Resource Sheet on page 58)
Pencil
Aim
For each *detective squad* to compile a full report with all crime details complete before the other detective squads do.

---

43 Team-building Activities for Key Stage 2
© Gavin Middlewood and Andrew Debenham

Hint: Successful teams should observe which cones have been tried already.

Extension: This can be repeated over a larger area.

Foxes and rabbits

You are in a group of foxes and have been set a challenge by the King of all Foxes, Ferdinand the Third, to catch rabbits for his dinner. He's feeling hungry, so you'll have to be quick. You are going to need to plan as a team how you will catch the rabbits as quickly as possible ...

Focus
Agility, problem-solving
Number of players
One team of 4 *foxes* at a time within a whole group of 15-30
Equipment
Coloured bands or bib
Stopwatch
Aim
For the *foxes* to catch all of the *rabbits* as quickly as possible.

Instructions

1. The teacher must select four children to become the *foxes*. They are distinguished by the coloured bands.

2. The rest of the group are the *rabbits*. The rabbits must each tuck a coloured band (or bib) in the back of their shorts or tracksuit bottoms and spread out around the playing area.

3. The foxes must next try to catch the *tails* (bands) of the rabbits. Foxes may move around as quickly as they wish. However, rabbits can move only by jumping with two feet together. Rabbits should sit down as soon as their tail is caught. The teacher should allow the foxes 2 minutes of planning time to discuss tactics before the activity begins.

4. When all of the tails have been caught, the teacher informs the foxes of the time taken. This becomes their score.

5. The activity is next repeated with another group of foxes, who must attempt to beat the time set previously.

Hint: Successful groups of foxes may decide to work in particular zones of the area or pair off to 'corner' the rabbits.

Marrow for the barrow

The local village is alive with excitement, as 'The 53rd Greendale Garden Fair' is soon to take place. With just a day to go, you and your fellow villagers' plans to enter the annual 'Mighty Marrow Contest' have been plunged into disarray. Gale-force winds have scattered your marrows all over the fields and you haven't long to gather them up ready for the fair. Time to start collecting!

Instructions

1. *The gale wreaks havoc* as the different-coloured *marrows* (beanbags) are scattered all around the playing area. The different colours are worth different amounts, but the children should not yet know how much each is worth.

2. Teams need to divide themselves up into pairs in order to make the *wheelbarrows* for the game. Wheelbarrows are made with one person standing up and holding onto the ankles of their partner, who walks using their hands to form the front.

3. When play begins, each team may send out only one barrow at a time. As soon as that barrow has collected a marrow, they should return to their team. A new barrow can then be sent out.

4. Play ends when all the marrows have been collected. The teacher can then reveal the monetary value of the different colours and teams can calculate how much they have earned for the fair.

Focus
Agility, balance, communication
Number of players
4-30, divided into teams of 2, 4 or 6
Equipment
Beanbags
Aim
For teams to collect as many *marrows* (beanbags) as they can using human wheelbarrows to pick up one marrow at a time and carry it back to their *house*.

Extension: Cones and benches can be used to form obstacles.

The great escape

It is 1942 and you have been taken as prisoners to a POW camp. However, Escape Officer General McQueen has planned a cunning escape. He proposes that whilst the rest of the prisoners play a football match against the guards, you and your group dig your way to freedom. You will need to start burrowing under the shower block, then over the water pipes and finally under the barbed-wire fence …

Focus
Cooperation, control of movement, agility
Number of players
4-6
Equipment
Large PE balls
Benches
Mats
Aim
To move as a group with the ball whilst negotiating a series of challenges in the quickest time possible.

Instructions

1. A course should be laid out consisting of an empty space followed by a bench and, finally, a PE mat.

2. Players will need to form a line. The first challenge is to *burrow under the showers*. This requires the children to take their *rock* (large PE ball) and pass it over their heads and through their legs alternately until it reaches the back of the line. When the last person receives the rock, they should run to the front. This process is repeated until the group reaches the *pipes* (bench).

3. The players then should straddle the bench, passing the rock between their legs along the top of the bench without it falling off. Should the rock fall off, players must return it to the beginning of the pipes.

43 Team-building Activities for Key Stage 2
© Gavin Middlewood and Andrew Debenham

4. After negotiating the pipes, the group progress to the *barbed-wire fencing* (PE mat). As each child gets to the mat they must sit on their bottoms and 'bottom-shuffle' across the mat and, as they do so, pass the rock over their heads to the child behind. If a child stands up, the group must return to the start of the fencing.

5. As soon as the whole group has left the fence, then the *prisoners are free* and the activity is complete.

Extension: Divide the class into groups competing against one another. It can also be set against the clock — *if the prisoners do not complete their escape in time*, then the escape will be rumbled and the firing squad awaits!

© Gavin Middlewood and Andrew Debenham

Jailbreak

Uh oh, there's a new sheriff in town! Up until now, you and your gang of desperadoes, known locally as 'The Lollipop Kids', have been running the show here in Tombstone, Arizona. However, after a long battle with Sheriff Billy Baggem you now find yourselves locked up in the tiny corridor of the town jail with a pair of 'six-shooters' pointed at you. As the day of 'baddie-bashing' takes its toll, the sheriff drops off to sleep and you notice a set of keys hanging on a hook at the end of the corridor. Can you pass the keys along the line to your accomplice waiting outside the window, or will you wake the sleeping sheriff?

Instructions

1. Children need to form a line standing on the bench.

2. The first child in the line places the beanbag under their chin.

3. All children, including the one with the beanbag, now need to place their hands on their heads. These cannot be removed until the challenge is completed.

4. *The prisoners* must now devise ways of passing *the key* to the end of the line without using their hands or letting the keys touch the bench or floor.

5. Once the last in line has received the key, they can drop it off the end of the bench, allowing the teacher to *open the door and release the captives*.

Focus
Cooperation, balance, problem-solving
Number of players
3-7
Equipment
Bench
Beanbag
Aim
To pass the beanbag from one end of the line to the other without using your hands, stepping from the bench or letting the beanbag touch the bench or the floor.

Hint: Chins, knees or feet could all be used to pass the beanbag.

The king's ransom

Your name is Phil Fog and you are on a mission to travel around the world in less than 80 days so that you can beat the record set by your great-uncle. So far you've negotiated the hardest part – getting from London to Dover without delays – and your passage across Central and Eastern Europe has been smooth. However, you've now run into trouble in Asia. You have strayed into land belonging to the King of Persia without asking for his permission. As punishment, his soldiers have kidnapped your travelling companion, Wanda Farr, and they won't let her go until you pay a ransom. The King wants 26 gifts, each beginning with a different letter of the alphabet. He's so angry that he won't open his door to you … so they must be able to fit through his keyhole!

Focus
Problem-solving
Number of players
Minimum of 4 players, divided into pairs
Equipment
Quoit (represents the keyhole)
Paper and pencil
Aim
To find 26 items that each begin with a different letter of the alphabet. These must be able to fit through the quoit.

Instructions

1. This activity must take place in a room that has lots of small items (eg, a school classroom).

2. Teams should list the letters of the alphabet vertically on their sheet of paper.

3. Teams must look around the room for items that would fit through the *keyhole* (quoit), aiming to find one for each letter.

4. When the task ends, teams may be required to prove that each item fits. Other teams are allowed to 'challenge' if they disagree.

Mission to Mars

AD 2106 ... Houston, Texas. You are about to launch your spaceship, Destiny 62, into space with the aim of becoming the first humans to land on planet Mars. However, to reach your destination, you and your fellow astronauts must overcome a series of challenges which will severely test your space navigation skills ...

Focus
Balance, cooperation
Number of players
4 or more players, divided into pairs
Equipment
Hoops
Mats or coned area
Aim
For each pair to pass the stages of the mission without having to visit the *space station* 3 times or more.

Instructions

1. Each pair must form a *spaceship* by standing opposite each other and placing their hands upon each other's shoulders.

2. The pairs begin their *mission* by moving around *space* (the playing area). However, if they let go of each other's shoulders or accidentally bump into another pair, they will need to visit the *space station* (the matted or coned area). At the space station, the children can repair their spaceship by performing 10 star jumps before rejoining the game and *recommencing their mission.*

3. After 2-3 minutes, the teacher should stop the children and inform them that *the ship's radar isn't working properly.* One child in each pair should close their eyes, and the mission continues.

43 Team-building Activities for Key Stage 2
© Gavin Middlewood and Andrew Debenham

4. Instruction 3 should then be repeated as *the radar is now malfunctioning on the opposite side of the ship* instead. This time, the other child should close their eyes and be guided.

5. The good news is that the radar is fine now. However, the bad news is that there is *turbulence*. Children can now see, but need to bounce their way around the playing area, again without letting go of each other or bumping.

6. *Turbulence is getting worse!* Players now must hop around on one leg only.

7. *You have nearly reached Mars.* However, the planet is protected by some *shooting stars*! Pairs can move about as normal, but this time they must avoid the hoops being rolled across the playing area by the teacher. Pairs who get hit must go to the space station; at the space station, children can repair their spaceship by performing 10 star jumps before rejoining the game.

8. *The mission to Mars is complete, but did you get there alive?* If your spaceship visited the space station fewer than three times, then you are heroes who will go down in history! If your spaceship had to visit the space station three times or more, then the ship unfortunately ended up crashing and plunging out of the galaxy!

Extension: *Mission to Mars* can be played with classes divided into of teams of three or four.

Space race

Your spaceship, Columbus 3, is returning to planet Earth when it suddenly runs out of power. You are still 500,000 miles from home and your dinner will be getting cold! Astronaut Zak Connor, who never listened in maths lessons, has miscalculated the number of hyperdrive energy crystals required for the journey. Vice-captain William Bartzog remembers that there are some spare crystals at the back of the spaceship. But who will be brave enough to get them?

Focus
Problem-solving, balance
Number of players
2-5
Equipment
Mats
Beanbags or quoits
Aim
To transport the *crystals* (beanbags) across the 'danger area' to your team as quickly as possible.

Instructions

1. Two mats should be placed upon the floor, separated by a gap of approximately 5 metres. The *crystals* (beanbags or quoits) should be piled on one of the mats, representing the *storage area*.

2. The team must base themselves at *the door to the spaceship* (the opposite mat). They will need to travel *outside the spaceship* (the gap between the mats) and back, transporting the crystals. Groups can send only one person at a time, and this player must keep their hands and feet on the floor at all times during crossing, otherwise *they will be sucked away into outer space*.

3. Groups should also be informed that the crystals are highly *radioactive* and *unstable*. Members can carry only one crystal at a time, and they must not carry them in their hands.

4. The activity is over when all of the crystals have been transported or when the time period has elapsed.

Extension: This can be made harder by increasing the gap between the mats.

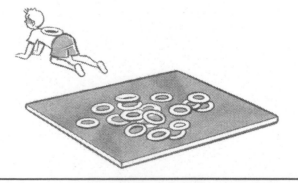

43 Team-building Activities for Key Stage 2
© Gavin Middlewood and Andrew Debenham

Staircases from hell

You've been imprisoned in London's dungeon for over 10 years, guarded day and night by Chief Security Guard, Chloe Z Lock. However, age has caught up with her, and last night she died in her sleep. The escape route is clear but the staircase out is old and rotted. Not every plank of wood will take your weight. Tread carefully …

Focus
Cooperation
Number of players
Up to 4 teams of 5 (maximum) players
Equipment
Hoops
Cones
Beanbags
Aim
To move along the *staircase* (line of hoops), throwing the beanbag into the hoops in as few throws as possible.

Instructions

1. The game grid must be set up as in the diagram below. Up to four groups can participate at one time, each starting in the areas labelled *dungeon chamber*.

2. Groups must decide upon the order in which they will *escape*, as only one group member can go at a time.

3. The first child can begin moving along the *steps* (hoops). Moves are made by throwing the beanbag into a hoop in front. If the beanbag lands in the next hoop, then the child can move one space forward. However, the child may decide to 'gamble' and aim for the second or third hoop. If they are successful, then fewer moves will be required. However, if the child misses the hoop, they must return to the dungeon chamber and start again in last position for their team.

4. The teams should keep count of their total number of moves until they all arrive in the *home area* (middle). If necessary, the teacher can appoint some children to serve as referees.

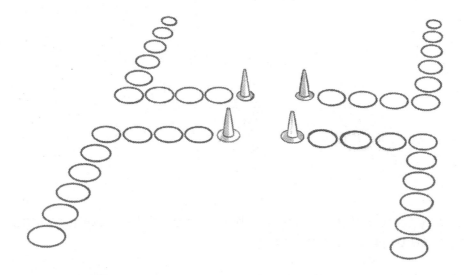

Extension: Keep reducing the maximum number of moves for each team.

Theseus and the Minotaur

It is many centuries ago, on the island of Crete, and you crouch nervously underground in the dark corridor listening to the sounds of battle as Theseus and the Minotaur slug it out! Slash! Ping! Crash! Aaaagghh! Silence follows ... the sound of footsteps steadily gets louder. Will it be Theseus whisking you to safety? Or, on the other hand, are you simply going to become 'dessert' for the Minotaur? To your relief, Theseus appears, ready to escort you to safety from this labyrinth of hell. No one has ever escaped before, but Theseus has a ball of string in his hand. Does he have a plan?

Focus
Problem-solving, communication
Number of players
3-6
Equipment
Skipping ropes
Aim
To transport the whole group through the *labyrinth* (maze of cones) without anyone touching the cones or leaving the maze.

Instructions

1. The *labyrinth* (maze) should be set up using cones.

2. The group should be given the skipping ropes and have 3-5 minutes to plan their strategies for negotiating the maze.

3. All but one member of the group (*Theseus*) should be blindfolded.

4. The group must be given a set time period by the teacher to negotiate the labyrinth, depending on its difficulty.

Hint: The easiest way to complete this is for the non-blindfolded child to lead their group and use the rope to guide team-mates.

Extension: Benches could be placed along the course that the children must step over without touching.

---

43 Team-building Activities for Key Stage 2
© Gavin Middlewood and Andrew Debenham

Volcanic eruption

It is AD 79 and a rumbling can be heard outside the great city of Pompeii, in the Roman Empire. No, it is not Emperor Titus's stomach! Mount Vesuvius has erupted and a deadly lava flow is about to descend upon your city. Your group can save themselves by climbing upon the great stone columns of the city. But are there enough to go around?

Instructions

1. The group are informed of the number of *stone columns* (number of limbs permitted to touch the floor) available to them. There should always be one stone column less than the number of group members.

Focus
Balance, cooperation, problem-solving
Number of players
4-6
Equipment
One mat per group
Aim
To keep control of a group balance with as few limbs touching the mat as possible.

2. The group should plan and practise their group balance in preparation for the arrival of *the deadly lava flow*. They may not pick up anyone above their shoulders, owing to *the clouds* of *suffocating volcanic dust*.

3. Upon the teacher's signal, the children should get into position to form their group balance. They must hold this balance for a full 8 seconds until *the lava subsides*.

Extension: This task can be made harder by asking the group to retain their balance for a longer period. The number of stone columns available can also be reduced.

Safety Note: The children should be reminded that normal gymnastic mats are not crash mats, and so they should take care to not drop group members.

Walk the plank

It is 1492 and you are world-famous explorer Christopher Columbus in search of new lands and treasures. However, as the supplies have run dry, mutiny has broken out! The crew decides that it is your fault and that you and your senior officers are to be cast adrift in a small boat. For their amusement they blindfold you and sabotage the plank. Do you trust all of the voices you can hear?

Instructions

1. Inform all children that in order to reach the boat, they must walk to the other end of the *plank* without falling down any of the *holes*, as represented by the equipment spaced out on the bench.

2. The group must then nominate one member to be the first to *walk the plank*!

3. This person must be blindfolded and should attempt to successfully complete their journey by listening to the instructions of their fellow group members.

4. Children must not touch any of the obstacles, otherwise they automatically become *shark bait* and are out of the game.

5. Continue activity until all group members have had a go.

Focus
Cooperation, communication, balance
Number of players
2 or more
Equipment
One bench
Quoits
Beanbags
Skipping ropes
Blindfolds
Aim
To guide each member of the group from one end of the *plank* (bench) to the other without touching any of the obstacles.

Extension: Two benches can be placed together at right angles to create a more challenging course.

Flapping around

On a class trip to the countryside, you spot a rather interesting, multi-coloured butterfly. 'Hey, that's the one I've seen in the newspaper!' cries Eleanor Jackson, the class science expert. 'And there's a £10,457 reward for anyone who finds it undamaged!' interrupts Tommy Francis, the class maths expert. Your group decide to capture this precious insect as you care lots about wildlife and, besides, the money would be nice …

Instructions

1. Each player is given a *butterfly flapper*.

2. The course needs to be marked out using skipping ropes and the *butterfly* (balloon) placed at the start.

3. The players need to work together to direct the butterfly along the course using their flappers to provide air propulsion.

Focus
Cooperation, problem-solving
Number of players
2-4
Equipment
Inflated balloon
One piece of A4-size card per child
Skipping ropes
Aim
To move the balloon from one end of the course to the other without touching it.

Hint: Players may position themselves to the left of, to the right of and behind the butterfly in order to control its movement effectively.

Extension: The course may be made harder if the players have to keep the butterfly within a narrow channel. Also, the task could end with the group having to finish off by flapping the butterfly into a bucket.

Hunger at 1,500 feet

You and your team of extreme thrillseekers are scaling yet another sheer mountain face, this time in the Atlas Mountains. You are halfway through the ascent and at a crucial point with the whole team needing to hang firmly onto the rope. Suddenly there is a loud call from the back.

'What's up?!' you shout. 'It's Matt Black and he's not going on until he gets a snack!' Matt is diabetic and he needs to eat now. Your problem is that the required rucksack is at the front of the line. Can you get it back to Matt (without letting go of the rope) before he becomes too weak to hold on?

Focus
Cooperation, balance
Number of players
3-7
Equipment
Bench
Hoop
Long skipping rope
Aim
To move the hoop from one end of the line to the other without letting go of the rope or stepping from the bench (*mountain face*).

Instructions

1. Ask the children to stand in line on the PE bench.

2. Tell the children to grasp the rope with both hands.

3. Place a hoop over the first child's raised arm.

4. Instruct the children to pass this *rucksack* to the back of the line without stepping from the bench or letting go of the rope.

Extension: Matt Black could be informed that he then has to return the rucksack to its original owner. The task can be made more difficult by passing a number of rucksacks.

'Lost' in the Pacific

You are travelling to Australia on an adventure holiday when storms strike and your pilot needs to make an emergency landing on a small island in the Pacific Ocean. Needing to get help quickly for the injured, you and your fellow passengers resolve to try to relay an urgent message to a plane that happens to be passing overhead. Just time to clamber onto the wing of the plane ...

Instructions

1. The bench needs to be turned upside down by the children to show that *the plane has crashed*.

2. All of the children in the group must stand on the bench.

3. The teacher provides each child with a word card.

4. The children must work out what the phrase is.

5. To complete the task, they should help each other move into the correct place on the bench without touching the floor. Children are not allowed to simply exchange word cards.

Focus
Cooperation, balance, problem-solving
Number of players
4-7
Equipment
Bench
Word cards (Resource Sheet on page 59)
Aim
For the group to put themselves in order without falling *from the wing of the plane* (bench).

Extension: This activity can be timed, with specified penalties being incurred each time a child touches the floor.

Safety Note: It is advisable for children/adults to hold each end of the bench to prevent it from tipping.

Super-glue undo

It's time for the local country-dancing festival to begin, and you and all your fellow dancers have now crossed arms ready for your first dance together. Unfortunately, you've also been making decorative floral hats for the dance using super-glue, and as soon as you join hands you all realize that you are stuck together. The ambulance arrives, but you must untangle yourselves before you can get in it!

Focus
Cooperation, problem-solving
Number of players
3 or more
Equipment
Quoits
Aim
For players to untangle their crossed arms and form a circle without letting go of the quoits.

Instructions

1. The players need to form a circle with each child holding a quoit in their right hand.

2. Each child must cross their right arm over their left arm.

3. Using their left hand each child must take hold of the quoit now available on their right-hand side.

4. Children must work together to uncross their arms whilst maintaining a firm grip on the quoits.

Extension: This task can be made more difficult by increasing the number of players.

Alien communication

An alien spacecraft hovers above the Earth and all normal forms of communication have broken down. A final chance to make contact before the aliens disappear lies with your group. You are to be given an important message to send to the UFO, but they are such a long way off that you will have to use your bodies in order for the symbols to be seen ...

Instructions

1. The children should divide their group up into *aliens* and *humans*. The humans will create the messages whilst the aliens write these down.

2. The aliens need to move to a viewing point away from the humans (a bench could be used).

3. The humans are given a message card containing five symbols. These children need to decide between them how they will use their bodies to convey the symbols to the aliens

4. As each symbol is made the aliens will attempt to draw them on the whiteboard.

5. Once all five symbols have been attempted the two parts of the group can meet together to compare their messages.

Focus
Non-verbal communication, problem-solving
Number of players
5-8 (minimum of 4 *humans* and one *alien*)
Equipment
Whiteboard and pen
Message card (Resource Sheet page 60)
Aim
For *the humans* to relay the given messages to *the aliens* using their bodies to create symbols.

Extension: The children can attempt to create their own symbols and messages.

Aztec temple

It is 1502 ... the time of the Aztec civilization. You are all currently working as master builders for Montezuma II. Unfortunately, though, it has been a disastrous harvest this year and, as a consequence, your leader is not happy. He decides that we all need to pay tribute to the Sun God with the building of a mighty new temple. Those who build the highest temple will receive great riches. Those who fail will be sacrificed in his honour. Get building!

Instructions

1. Each team must be given the same equipment (eg, 3-5 large PE balls, 4 beanbags, 4 quoits and 3 hoops). However, this may be varied depending on what is available.

2. The teams should be informed that they must use the given equipment to construct the tallest *Aztec temple* that they can. It must be self-supporting.

3. Once a team of builders declares that their temple is complete, the teacher can measure the height of the group's Aztec temple.

Focus
Problem-solving, cooperation
Number of players
Teams of 2-5 players
Equipment
Large PE balls
Beanbags
Quoits
Hoops
Metre sticks
Aim
To construct the tallest free-standing structure possible using the available equipment.

Extension: Equipment available can be increased to create more sophisticated temples.

43 Team-building Activities for Key Stage 2
© Gavin Middlewood and Andrew Debenham

Cave of doom

A school trip to the caves turns into a nightmare as your teacher's torch goes dead. 'Just put in a new battery!' cries Eleanor Jackson, the class science expert. However, your absent-minded teacher has forgotten to carry a spare. It's pitch-black and the exit is closing up, but at least you have some rope …

Instructions

1. Each player must hold the string and be blindfolded.

2. All players should be informed of the order that they need to organize themselves into (eg, alphabetical, age or height).

3. When the children are happy with their order, they should try to move as a group to the teacher by listening to the teacher's voice.

Focus
Cooperation, verbal and non-verbal communication
Number of players
5-10
Equipment
Skipping rope/string
One blindfold per child
Aim
Players must organize themselves into a specified order whilst blindfolded. Following this, they should try to reach the *safety* of the teacher.

Hint: If the players are finding this difficult, the teacher can *light a match* by allowing one player 10 seconds of vision.

Extension: This exercise can be made harder by allowing only non-verbal methods of communication (eg, clapping, whistling and foot-stamping).

Chance to dance

There's a hot new show on television! 'Chance to Dance' is the Saturday-night show that is taking the nation by storm every weekend. Contestants must dance their way through a series of challenges in order to become 'King' or 'Queen' of the dance floor. However, to your horror, you've just received news that you'll be appearing on this week's show. Your 'best mate', Dave, has entered you for the contest without you knowing! Why is this so bad? Well, you can't dance! Dave is rubbing his hands with glee. Can you learn fast and cause the joke to backfire?

Focus
Control of movement, communication
Number of players
Several teams of 2
Equipment
Resource sheet of dance moves (page 61) to perform
Aim
To learn and perform the moves for each round of the dance contest without making any mistakes.

Instructions

1. Children must form pairs to work in. One member should be the *dance teacher* whilst the other should be the *contestant*.

2. The dance teachers should be presented with the resource sheets. They must next work with the contestant to learn and practise the moves required for 'Round One'. When these have been learnt, the pair should work on the following rounds in order. These increase in difficulty.

3. At the teacher's discretion, the dance training should end, meaning it's now time for the 'Dance Off'. Dance teachers should watch the dancers perform each round. When a mistake is made, then that contestant is eliminated from the competition.

4. This continues until the final contestant remains. They are then crowned 'King' or 'Queen' of the dance floor.

Extension: Children can work with partners to synchronize their moves.

---

43 Team-building Activities for Key Stage 2
© Gavin Middlewood and Andrew Debenham

The crown jewels

You, criminal mastermind Turner Power, are about to pull off the crime of the century: stealing the crown jewels. Whilst you have managed to shut down the security cameras, your accomplice Jack Riddell has cracked the code to the safe. Right now the guards are cleverly being distracted as Naomi Anderton and Sophie Moss ask for directions to the Natural History Museum. However, as your team climbs the Tower of London, you notice rival gangs seizing upon this once-in-a-lifetime chance to get rich. A frantic race for the crown jewels begins …

Focus
Agility, problem-solving
Number of players
3-7 teams of 4-5
Equipment
Hoops
Beanbags
Aim
To have the greatest number of *crown jewels* (beanbags) when the teacher ends the challenge.

Instructions

1. 20-30 *crown jewels* (beanbags) should be placed inside the *Tower of London* (centre hoop).

2. The teams each begin in separate hoops at each side of the playing area. They must decide upon an order as only one member can be sent at a time, to steal *one jewel only*.

3. When the teacher begins the game, the first child must run to the Tower and steal a jewel for their team. This must be placed in that team's hoop before the next person goes.

4. Play continues until all of the jewels have been stolen. At this point, children must now steal from each other's hoops. They may not protect their previously stolen jewels from being taken.

5. When the teacher ends the game, the jewels are counted.

Hint: Teams should discuss which team's hoops they should steal from in order to win the challenge.

Codebreaker

Your team of archaeologists have travelled to Peru and followed a trail of clues that have led you to a hidden stone doorway in Machu Picchu. A sequence of ancient symbols carved into a rock face suggests that valuable treasures may be hidden in the cave behind. You push at the door and suddenly it springs open, allowing you to creep inside. No sooner are you in, but the door slams shut and you are trapped! You switch on the torch to find a keypad covered in mysterious symbols, but which ones will open the door? The batteries in your torch are running out fast and soon you will be in complete darkness. Can you and your fellow explorers work through the code before it is too late and you are trapped forever?!

Focus
Agility, problem-solving, communication
Number of players
3-5
Equipment
Calculators
Number sentences (see resource sheet on page 62)
Aim
To correctly relay a numerical message as quickly as possible.

Instructions

1. The class need to decide upon a *codebreaker*.
   This player will move to the opposite side of the playing area and switch on the calculator.

2. Upon the teacher's signal, the remaining players can look at the numerical message to send.

3. The group must decide how to efficiently send the message to the codebreaker. They may each cross the playing area only one at a time.

4. As each player arrives with part of the message, the codebreaker enters it into their *micro-computer* (calculator).

43 Team-building Activities for Key Stage 2
© Gavin Middlewood and Andrew Debenham

5. When the codebreaker has all of the message, they press the = key to reveal an answer.

6. The codebreaker then needs to take the answer to the teacher to discover if it is correct and whether *the code has been broken.*

Hint: If children feel they are capable of remembering sets of numbers rather than single digits, then they will complete the task much quicker. However, this also increases the risk of making mistakes with the code.

Extension: This activity can be made harder by introducing longer and more complicated number sentences. Also, you can try using a larger area where the codebreaker is a long way from the rest of the class. For groups especially skilled at maths, try omitting the calculator.

Desert gold

You have been in the desert for months fighting a great war on behalf of your country, but your army has split into two factions. There's been word that you are now in a region where precious and ancient gold has been left untouched for centuries. Have the months of toil and sweat been for nothing? Or can you beat your rivals to the desert gold?!

Instructions

1. The class needs to be divided into two teams. These should be distinguished by different-coloured bands (or bibs) tucked into their waistbands at the back (tails).

2. The playing area should be split into two equal halves, with five cones spread out at the back of each team's territory. Three of the five cones must conceal a piece of *desert gold* (ball). There should be a marked-out area in front of the cones so that the cones cannot be defended too closely.

3. The teams need to try to capture the gold at the back of their opponents' territory. Once a piece of gold is captured, they should shout 'Desert Gold!' and then return to their team unchallenged with the gold. However, if the cone is empty, they must visit *army prison* (see Instruction 4).

4. Soldiers can move anywhere, but if their tail is removed they must visit army prison, which is in a coned area next to the desert. The tail is then placed outside the prison. Prisoners can pick up their tail and return to the game only when they have performed the *prison duty* of 50 tuck jumps.

5. Soldiers are not allowed to touch or push opponents. Anyone caught doing so must visit the army prison and perform a prison duty of 50 tuck jumps before being allowed to return to the game.

Focus
Problem-solving, agility, communication
Number of players
2 teams of at least 3 players each
Equipment
6 yellow tennis balls (to represent the *gold*)
Cones or markers
Coloured bands or bibs
Aim
For your *army* to find all 3 pieces of the *desert gold* before the opposing team does.

Hints: Successful teams should discuss how they are going to attack and defend the territories. Members also should plan how to tell each other about where the pieces of gold are.

Extension: This game can be played within a specified time period. It can also be made more challenging by introducing more 'false cones' that don't conceal gold, meaning that team members need to communicate more information about gold whereabouts to each other.

Hole in the wall

You are holidaying in San Francisco with friends when suddenly the room starts moving! EARTHQUAKE! Your hotel building begins to collapse around you and there's no time to get out. You crouch and attempt to take shelter from the falling bricks. A few minutes later, the earthquake subsides and your group are relieved to see that no one is hurt. However, you must leave quickly as the building is unstable. A hole in the wall lies in front of you ...

Focus
Cooperation, problem-solving
Number of players
4-6
Equipment
Hoops
Skipping ropes
Aim
To transport all the group through the *two holes* (hoops) without touching the hoop edges or falling into the gap between the ropes.

Instructions

1. A gap of approximately 1 metre should be made using the skipping ropes. One member is permitted to cross it and hold the hoop. This must be held at least 50 centimetres above the gap throughout the task.

2. Each group must attempt to transport its members through the hoop without touching it. No one may jump or dive through the hoop. The final member of the group is permitted to walk straight past.

3. *The next hole in the wall is higher.* The group should repeat the exercise with the hoop raised to 70 centimetres.

Hint: The largest/strongest children should be sent first and last.

Extension: The building is falling fast. Groups are against the clock.

Frog swap

It's exciting times down at the pond. Frog TV are filming a new reality television show called 'Frog Swap' in which neighbouring frogs exchange homes for a week in order to experience what life is like on other lily pads. Your family – Freddy, Freda and Frankie – have been chosen to star in the first episode. You will need to hop along to the neighbouring lily pads without bumping into the family that's coming the other way!

Instructions

1. The group needs to set out a line of eight hoops to mark out the *lily pads*. (Cones may also be used.)

2. The group should divide themselves into two *families* and then position themselves into hoops at opposite ends of the line. Each family is distinguished by different-coloured bibs.

3. The group must then work together to exchange places so that the families finish at the end opposite to where they started.

4. *Frogs* should move forwards towards their destination and although they may jump over their neighbouring frogs they are permitted to do so only if there is a spare lily pad beyond them. Frogs can never move backwards, and only one frog may visit a lily pad at any one time.

Hint: Players should be allowed an opportunity to discuss their starting positions and movements beforehand.

Extension: This task can be made harder by increasing the family sizes and adjusting the number of lily pads.

Focus
Problem-solving
Number of players
6
Equipment
Hoops or cones
Coloured bands or bibs
Aim
For the 2 families of *frogs* to exchange places on the *lily pads*.

Doctor How and the Darlets

The year is 2045, and Doctor How has turned evil. He is using his time-travelling powers to create chaos in the world, such as causing children to take over schools and Crystal Palace to win the FA Cup. You are a team of Darlets who must work together to defeat Doctor How and take over his time machine, Travis, so that you can travel back to 2015 and stop the timelord from bringing about the world's destruction …

Instructions

1. Children need to first pair up to make a *Darlet*. To do this, the pair must stand inside the hoop and hold it with their hands. The front person must then be blindfolded.

2. Darlets must walk around the playing area. If they bump into another Darlet, they must visit the *Darlet Factory* and complete three synchronized jumps before rejoining the game.

3. For the next stage, *Doctor How* (the teacher) *fires their laser gun* (rolling quoits into the playing area) at the Darlets. If one hits a Darlet, then that pair must visit the Darlet Factory.

Focus
Cooperation, communication
Number of players
Pairs within a larger group of 10-30
Equipment
Hoops – half as many as there are players, and at least 7 additional hoops for spelling out letters.
Several quoits
Blindfolds
Crates or cones
Aim
To pass each stage of the challenge and reach the *time machine* without *visiting the Darlet Factory more than twice.*

43 Team-building Activities for Key Stage 2
© Gavin Middlewood and Andrew Debenham

4. The Darlets must each pick up the *laser bullets* (quoits) and dispose of these in one of the *Darlet Dustbins* (crates), without bumping into one another.

5. For the final challenge, Darlets must communicate with each other and form the word TIME, using hoops for each letter. Creating this message will *open up the time machine and help save the world.* (Children may also spell out the word using their bodies.)

6. The challenge then should be repeated with children taking turns being blindfolded.

Extension: Making the playing area smaller will increase the chance of the Darlets bumping into one another.

Landslide

Your group trek across the Rocky Mountains is rudely interrupted by a huge grizzly bear who decides to chase you away from her cubs, and towards the edge of a narrow precipice. As you teeter on the edge, the ground gives way and you and the rest of your group tumble to the bottom of a small gorge defined by unconquerable steep slopes. Fortunately, one of your party is a member of the United Kingdom Jigsaw Team. If you follow his instructions, you may be able to piece together a precarious tower from the fallen boulders, enabling you and your group to climb out of your rocky prison!

Instructions

1. One child needs to be nominated the jigsaw expert. This person becomes *The Keeper of The Rules.*

2. The remaining children must attempt to build a *tower/bridge* from the hoops whilst adhering to *The Rules*. No one is allowed to see The Rules apart from *The Keeper*.

3. The Rules are as follows:
   - No reds are to be placed next to each other.
   - A yellow must be followed by a blue.
   - Two consecutive blues must be followed by a red.
   - You cannot start or finish the bridge with a yellow.
   - The sequence 'blue-yellow-red' is forbidden!

4. Each child may carry only one single hoop (*rock*) in a single turn.

Focus
Problem-solving
Number of players
3-5
Equipment
4 yellow hoops
4 blue hoops
3 red hoops
A set of rules (see below)
Aim
To construct a *tower/bridge* that spans the playing area whilst adhering to 'The Rules'.

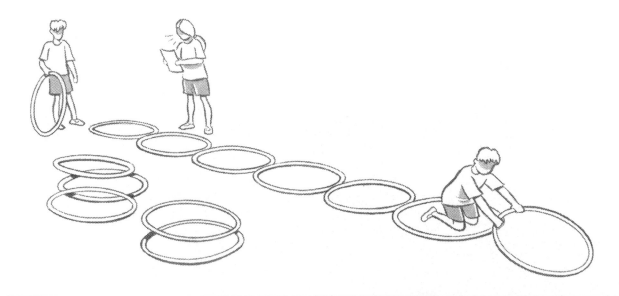

43 Team-building Activities for Key Stage 2
© Gavin Middlewood and Andrew Debenham

5. Children must place the next hoop in the line by travelling along the extending bridge, placing it in line and then returning back along the bridge to allow the next person with the next hoop to take their turn.

6. Once the bridge is complete, all children may travel along the bridge, providing that it is completed within The Rules.

Resource Tip: If the hoops are not available in the colours listed above, then other colours can be substituted. Also, adding an extra red hoop will make the task much easier.

A quiet life

You all are training to become elite Tibetan monks, but 'the road to enlightenment is littered with many obstacles.' When you arrive at the monastery for your first day's training, your head is shaved and you are told that you must undertake a vow of silence. Each trainee is assigned to one of four houses. You are told which house you are in and then instructed to line up with its other members. This would be easy … if you were allowed to speak!

Focus
Non-verbal communication, teamwork
Number of players
12-30
Equipment
House cards (Resource Sheet on page 63)
Aim
To assemble into predetermined groups without speaking.

Instructions

1. The children should be lined up outside the playing area and informed that they are not allowed to speak to each other.

2. As they enter, they should each be given a House Card and told that they cannot show this card to anyone.

3. All trainee monks must now arrange themselves into their correct Houses, as indicated on each of their cards.

4. Once the trainees have formed groups, the teacher should instruct them that they must line up according to the ordinal number on their card. They must still not show this card to anyone.

5. The first group to assemble themselves correctly (and without speaking) wins!

Extension: Blindfolding some monks will increase difficulty.

43 Team-building Activities for Key Stage 2
© Gavin Middlewood and Andrew Debenham

The Olympic curling final

After years of dedication, you and your ace team of curlers have finally made it to the Olympic Team Curling Final. Stadium announcer Vince Lennon Junior is at the mike. 'And now from Montreal, Canada, for all those in attendance … and for the millions watching around the world … LET'S GET READY TO CURR-L-L … ! … Oh no! The lights are out, folks!' Panic follows, but the organizers decide that the event must go on. Time to curl … in darkness!

Instructions

1. Set out the target area (see below). Ideally, different-coloured hoops should be used for each row.

2. One child from each pair has four turns at *curling the stone* (rolling the ball) towards the target area whilst blindfolded. Partners can aid the roller by giving advice concerning pace and direction.

3. After the four rolls, a score can be calculated for each pair: one point for the front hoop, two for the second row, three for the third and four for any ball finishing in the back line of hoops.

4. The balls are collected and the game is repeated, this time with children swapping roles with their partners.

5. The combined scores of the pairs decide the winning team.

Extension: The distance to the target area can be lengthened.

Focus
Communication, cooperation
Number of players
Pairs, with up to 4 pairs competing in one game
Equipment
Hoops
Tennis ball or similar
Blindfolds
Aim
For children to roll the ball towards the target area, aiming to score as many points as possible for their team.

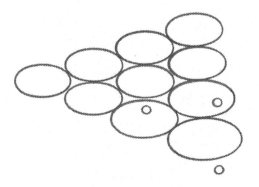

The seafood shuffle

Many years ago, you and your family of crabs made your home in an old WWII submarine. Unfortunately, every time there is a storm it gets pushed further over the edge of an underwater ledge on which it balances. Last night was the biggest storm that any crab can remember. This morning you awoke feeling strangely seasick. The submarine is swaying up and down. Clearly, it is about to crash down into the deep and it is time for you to leave. Suddenly, there is a loud clang ... the exit hatch has slammed shut!

Focus
Coordination, communication
Number of players
Several teams of 2
Equipment
Benches
Hoop
Skipping ropes
Aim
To successfully negotiate the course whilst being 'locked into position' with a partner.

Instructions

1. An obstacle course must be arranged using benches (*submarines*) and skipping ropes (*seaweed*), ending with a hoop (*hatch*).

2. Children need to stand back-to-back with a partner.

3. Pairs can now link arms. Correct positioning will see their elbows hooked together behind them with their hands returning to a forward position. They are now *a crab*.

4. Children can practise moving and turning as crabs.

5. Upon a given signal, crabs will attempt to successfully negotiate the obstacle course. To make their final escape they will have to work out how to lift the *hatch* and climb into the *open water*.

Extension: Two benches joined at sharp angles will increase difficulty.

43 Team-building Activities for Key Stage 2
© Gavin Middlewood and Andrew Debenham

Submarine commander

It is World War II and you are the commander of an Allied submarine. Your task is to escort shipping as it travels across the Atlantic Ocean. This has been relatively simple – until now! Somehow, enemy frogmen have managed to lay mines across the entrance to Portsmouth Harbour. It is pitch-black, and if any of the ships hit a mine they will be destroyed. With your sonar equipment, it is up to you to inform the ships' captains of the location of the mines and to save as many ships as you can.

Focus
Communication, cooperation
Number of players
2-8
Equipment
Cones/markers
Blindfolds
Aim
For players to cross the playing area without touching any of the markers and whilst wearing a blindfold.

Instructions

1. The cones (or markers) should be randomly laid out in *Portsmouth Harbour*.

2. The group needs to elect one member as *submarine captain*. The remaining players will be *ships coming into port*.

3. The *ships' captains* will be blindfolded and, upon a signal, they must attempt to cross the harbour without touching a *mine*. Should they do so they are deemed to have been *sunk*.

4. The submarine captain should then attempt to direct the ships into port using verbal instructions.

5. As soon as a ship reaches port, its captain may aid the submarine captain with instructions to other ships.

Hint: It is best to get one ship home as soon as possible so that the other ships can be assisted by the recently docked captain.

Survival of the caterpillars

You are a caterpillar. Yes, that's right – a caterpillar! But all is not right in the garden. Your evil human neighbours have decided to dig up the greenery and lay a patio. Therefore, it is time for you to vacate your dwelling. Can you wriggle your way in and out of the garden's obstacles before you are sliced in half?

Instructions

1. Create an obstacle course using the equipment.

2. The group then needs to form a *human caterpillar* by placing a large ball between each person.

3. The caterpillar should attempt to move without breaking up. The sections of the caterpillar need to remain tight so that the balls do not fall to the floor.

4. The caterpillar must attempt to reach its destination. Penalties are incurred each time a ball falls or a child touches a ball with their hands.

Focus
Cooperation, communication
Number of players
2-6
Equipment
Large balls
Assorted objects (eg, quoits, beanbags, benches and hoops)
Aim
For the group to move from one end of the *garden* (course) to the other without the balls falling *and the caterpillar breaking up.*

Extension: The obstacle course may be made more difficult as required. Courses that include turning demand a much higher degree of skill.

Treasure trove

You are in the Himalayas with a party of fellow explorers. You have not found a yeti, but you have unearthed a fantastic treasure trove and are in the process of taking it home. Unfortunately, as your lead member crosses the rickety bridge that links two mountain peaks, the bridge collapses. Your task is to somehow transport the precious and fragile treasure across to the lead member before nightfall …

Instructions

1. One player (the *lead member*) must cross to the bench (or mat) opposite them.

2. Next, all children must be told that the *rickety bridge* has collapsed.

3. The players must attempt to transport the *treasure* (equipment) across the gap between the benches. Children must not step off their bench, otherwise they *fall to their death!*

Focus
Problem-solving, cooperation
Number of players
3-5
Equipment
2 benches or mats
1 crate or small box of small, assorted objects (eg, quoits, balls, skipping ropes etc)
Aim
To transport as much *treasure* as possible to the lead member across the gap without dropping and therefore *destroying it.*

Hint: Throwing equipment over to the lead member is permitted, but if it is dropped it is out of the game. Also, the skipping ropes could be used to slide items along.

Extension: This can be tried again with a different variety of equipment (including the box itself) and a bigger gap between benches.

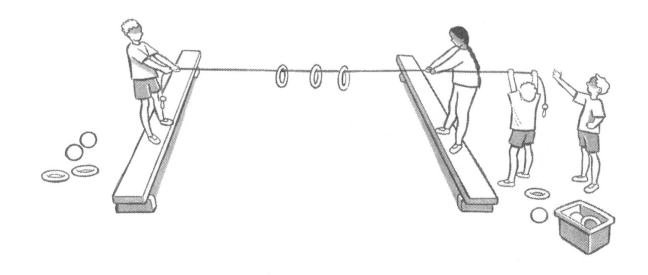

The unexploded bomb

Panic has broken out in the suburbs of Northampton. Builders in the area have found an unexploded bomb from World War II, and it needs to be defused. This would normally be an easy task for you and your work colleagues. After all, you are bomb-disposal experts who have years of experience behind you. However, this bomb is lying deep in a river. Moreover, it is highly unstable and will explode if dropped. The local residents have been evacuated and now it is up to you to extract the bomb from the river ...

Focus
Problem-solving, cooperation
Number of players
4-30, divided into groups of 4-6
Equipment
Crate or waste bin
PE mat or cones
Skipping ropes
Aim
To extract the *bomb* (crate) from the *river* (PE mat) without entering the river or directly touching the bomb.

Instructions

1. The *bomb* must be placed in the centre of the *river*. No player is allowed to enter the river throughout the task.

2. Teams are given two skipping ropes each to assist them.

3. The teacher must inform teams that the *residents' evacuation is complete* and that they may begin the task.

4. If the bomb is dropped at any time, it should be repositioned in the centre of the river and the team must start again.

Hint: Successful teams will use the skipping ropes simultaneously.

Extension: *The bomb is ticking.* The task has a set time period.

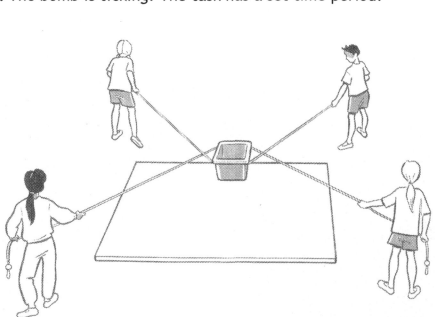

43 Team-building Activities for Key Stage 2
© Gavin Middlewood and Andrew Debenham

Island SOS

Photocopiable resource sheet (see page 8)

H	E	L	P

Q	U	I	C	K

R	E	S	C	U	E

T	R	A	P	P	E	D

Detective squad

Detective report

Criminal's name:
Age:
Occupation:
Location of crime:
Type of crime:
Weapon used:

43 Team-building Activities for Key Stage 2
© Gavin Middlewood and Andrew Debenham

'Lost' in the Pacific

Photocopiable resource sheet (see page 33)

OUR	PLANE	HAS	CRASHED

THIS	IS	A	BIG	EMERGENCY

DROP	SOME	FOOD	DOWN	TO	US

OUR	TWO	PILOTS	NEED

A	DOCTOR	URGENTLY

Alien communication

Photocopiable resource sheet (see page 35)

YEARS
5-6

43 Team-building Activities for Key Stage 2
© Gavin Middlewood and Andrew Debenham

Chance to dance

YEARS
5-6

Photocopiable resource sheet (see page 38)

These are suggested routines. However, the children may enjoy making up their own.

Round 1

4 side-steps left, 4 side-steps right, 2 star jumps.
Repeat.

Round 2

3 steps forward, 3 steps back, 2 side-steps left, clap hands once, 2 side-steps right, clap hands twice.

Round 3

5 hops on the right leg, 5 hops on the left leg, 2 spins, 3 side-steps left, 3 side-steps right, 2 jumps forward, 2 jumps back, 4 star jumps.

Round 4

3 star jumps, 6 side-steps left, 2 jumps, 6 side-steps right, 4 jumps, 3 spins, clap hands twice, 4 steps forward, 4 steps back, 5 hops on the left leg, 3 hops on the right leg.

© Gavin Middlewood and Andrew Debenham

Codebreaker

Photocopiable resource sheet (see page 40)

A. $2743652 \div 598258 =$

B. $7645399 \div 628122 =$

C. $5633233 \div 332232 =$

D. $6343456 \div 132132 =$

E. $3232323 \div 233233 =$

F. $7432 \times 321 - 50000 + 123321 =$

G. $65324 \times 44 - 40024 + 321132 =$

H. $100000 - 100000 + 10000 \div 20 =$

I. $101010 - 10101 + 1010 \div 1 =$

J. $25.5 + 25.5 + 2525.25 - 52.52 =$

A quiet life

Photocopiable resource sheet (see page 50)

House of the 1 shake **1**st	House of the 2 shakes **1**st	House of the 3 shakes **1**st	House of the 4 shakes **1**st
House of the 1 shake **2**nd	House of the 2 shakes **2**nd	House of the 3 shakes **2**nd	House of the 4 shakes **2**nd
House of the 1 shake **3**rd	House of the 2 shakes **3**rd	House of the 3 shakes **3**rd	House of the 4 shakes **3**rd
House of the 1 shake **4**th	House of the 2 shakes **4**th	House of the 3 shakes **4**th	House of the 4 shakes **4**th
House of the 1 shake **5**th	House of the 2 shakes **5**th	House of the 3 shakes **5**th	House of the 4 shakes **5**th
House of the 1 shake **6**th	House of the 2 shakes **6**th	House of the 3 shakes **6**th	House of the 4 shakes **6**th
House of the 1 shake **7**th	House of the 2 shakes **7**th	House of the 3 shakes **7**th	House of the 4 shakes **7**th